21st Century
Junior Library

INFOGRAPHICS:
INFLATION

Christina Hill

Econo-Graphics Jr.

Published in the United States of America by

CHERRY LAKE PUBLISHING GROUP
Ann Arbor, Michigan
www.cherrylakepublishing.com

Reading Adviser: Beth Walker Gambro, MS, Ed., Reading Consultant, Yorkville, IL
Photo Credits: © Cover, Page 1: ©z_wei/Getty Images; Page 9: ©AlexZel/Pixabay, ©Clker-Free-Vector-Images/Pixabay, ©OpenClipart-Vectors/Pixabay; Page 12: ©Rudzhan Nagiev/Getty Images,©Pixabay; Page 14: ©NPavelN/Getty Images, ©FGC/Shutterstock, ©Sira Anamwong/Shutterstock; Page 15: ©Carlos Insignares/Pixabay, ©Clker-Free-Vector-Images/Pixabay, ©Megan Rexazin/Pixabay, ©Mohamed Hassan/Pixabay,©OpenClipart-Vectors/Pixabay, ©Ricarda Mölck/Pixabay; Page 16: ©BRO Vector/Getty Images, ©Dzm1try/Shutterstock, ©Golden Sikorka/Shutterstock, ©Microba Grandioza/Shutterstock, ©pathdoc/Shutterstock, ©Seahorse Vector/Shutterstock, ©sub job/Shutterstock, ©SurfsUp/Shutterstock; Page 20: ©GraphicMama-team/Pixabay; Page 22: ©Mironova Iuliia/Shutterstock

Cherry Lake Press is an imprint of Cherry Lake Publishing Group.

Library of Congress Cataloging-in-Publication Data
Names: Hill, Christina, author.
Title: Infographics. Inflation / Christina Hill.
Other titles: Inflation
Description: Ann Arbor, Michigan : Cherry Lake Publishing, [2023] | Series: Econo-graphics Jr. | Includes bibliographical references and index. | Audience: Grades 2-3 | Summary: "How does inflation work? In the Econo-Graphics Jr. series, young readers will examine economy-related issues from many angles, all portrayed through visual elements. Income, budgeting, investing, supply and demand, global markets, inflation, and more are covered. Each book highlights pandemic-era impacts as well. Created with developing readers in mind, charts, graphs, maps, and infographics provide key content in an engaging and accessible way. Books include an activity, glossary, index, suggested reading and websites, and a bibliography"— Provided by publisher.
Identifiers: LCCN 2022037955 | ISBN 9781668919231 (hardcover) | ISBN 9781668920251 (paperback) | ISBN 9781668921586 (ebook) | ISBN 9781668922910 (pdf)
Subjects: LCSH: Inflation (Finance)—Juvenile literature.
Classification: LCC HG229 .H5495 2023 | DDC 332.4/1—dc23/eng/20220906
LC record available at https://lccn.loc.gov/2022037955
Cherry Lake Publishing Group would like to acknowledge the work of the Partnership for 21st Century Learning, a network of Battelle for Kids. Please visit http://www.battelleforkids.org/networks/p21 for more information.

Printed in the United States of America
Corporate Graphics

Before embracing a career as an author, **Christina Hill** received a bachelor's degree in English from the University of California, Irvine, and a graduate degree in literature from California State University, Long Beach. When she is not writing about various subjects from sports to economics, Christina can be found hiking, mastering yoga handstands, or curled up with a classic novel. Christina lives in sunny Southern California with her husband, two sons, and beloved dog, Pepper Riley.

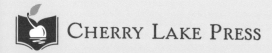

CONTENTS

What Is Inflation?   4

Cost-Push Inflation   8

Demand-Pull Inflation   10

Measures of Inflation   13

Inflation Pros and Cons   19

Activity   22
Learn More   23
Glossary   24
Index   24

WHAT IS INFLATION?

Inflation is when prices go up over time. Sometimes goods and services are in high **demand**. **Consumers** will pay more. This makes prices go up.

Deflation is the opposite of inflation. More goods and services are available than people demand. This makes prices go down.

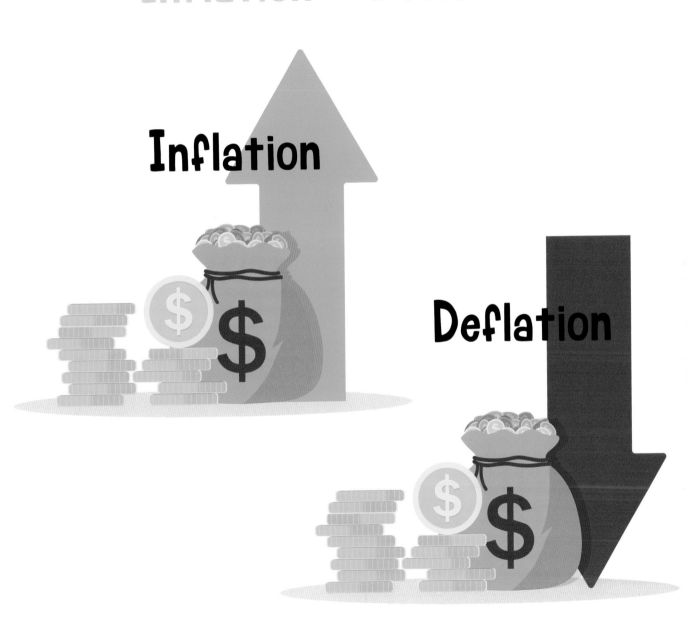

Inflation and the Average Cost of a McDonald's Big Mac

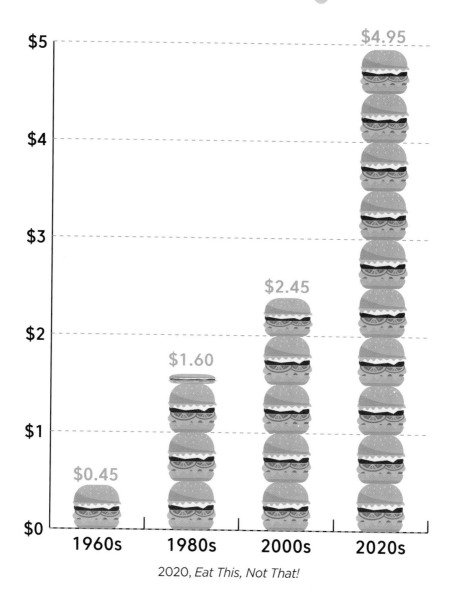

$5

$4.95

$4

$3

$2.45

$2

$1.60

$1

$0.45

$0

1960s 1980s 2000s 2020s

2020, *Eat This, Not That!*

Costs of a Big Mac Across the United States (2021)

Rates of inflation aren't the same across the country. The same burger costs more in different areas.

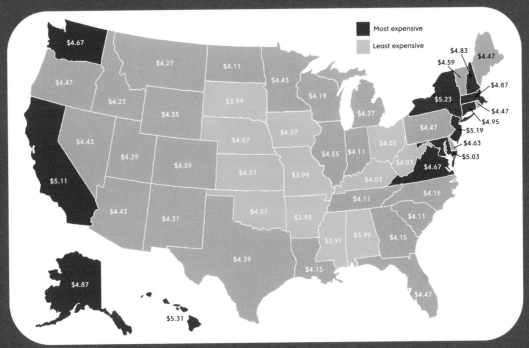

Most expensive
Least expensive

$4.67
$4.27
$4.11
$4.43
$4.83
$4.59
$4.47
$4.47
$4.23
$4.19
$4.87
$4.35
$3.99
$5.23
$4.43
$4.27
$4.47
$4.39
$4.07
$4.07
$4.47
$4.95
$5.11
$4.59
$4.07
$3.99
$4.55
$4.11
$4.03
$5.19
$4.03
$4.63
$5.03
$4.67
$4.43
$4.31
$4.07
$3.95
$4.03
$4.15
$3.91
$3.99
$4.11
$4.11
$4.39
$4.15
$4.15
$4.87
$5.31
$4.47

Cost Factors

- Real estate prices
- Employment rates
- Spending habits
- Product availability

COST-PUSH INFLATION

Sometimes prices go up because of the higher cost of **raw materials** and **wages**. These costs push up the prices. The supply goes down. But people still demand the products. This is called cost-push inflation.

Cost-Push Inflation

The cost of raw materials goes up.

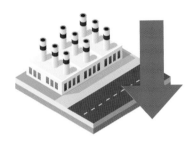

Factories have fewer materials. Production goes down.

Customers still demand the same amount.

The higher costs are passed to the customer as higher prices.

DEMAND-PULL INFLATION

Demand-pull inflation happens when demand suddenly goes up. There aren't enough goods to meet the demand. The high demand pulls up prices.

Apple's iPhone Prices

The Apple brand is in high demand. This inflates the price of each new phone that is released. This is an example of demand-pull inflation.

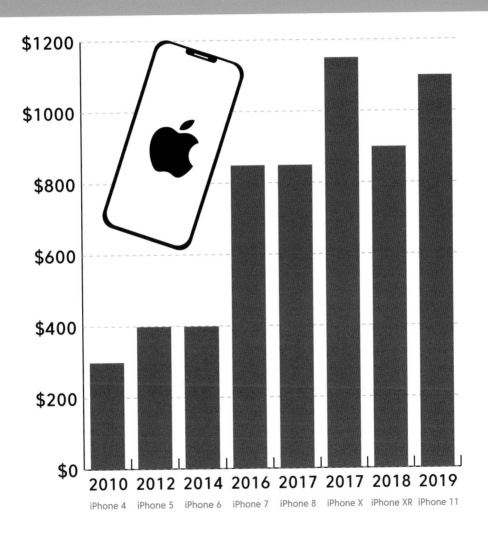

Year	2010	2012	2014	2016	2017	2017	2018	2019
Phone	iPhone 4	iPhone 5	iPhone 6	iPhone 7	iPhone 8	iPhone X	iPhone XR	iPhone 11

2019, Apple

Consumer Demand for PlayStation 5 Inflates Prices

- Demand for PS5 gaming consoles went up during the COVID-19 pandemic. More people were staying home. They played more video games. Stores sold out of the systems within seconds. There were not enough to keep up with the demand.

- As a result, people began buying and reselling PS5s. The prices inflated due to the low supply and high demand.

- Disc Version: $499; resold for $798.05; a 60% markup

- Digital Version: $399; resold for $759.22; a 90% markup

MEASURES OF INFLATION

One way to track inflation is with a price **index**. This chart shows the prices of goods and services over time.

The Consumer Price Index (CPI) shows the price of goods and services every month. The CPI can show price changes. It can show if the economy is healthy. It can show how much a dollar is worth.

The Producer Price Index (PPI) shows price changes from the seller. The PPI can forecast inflation. If the cost to make goods goes up, the prices will likely go up too.

Stagflation

Stagflation happens when both prices and unemployment go up.

The United States had a time of stagflation in the 1970s. Oil prices and shipping costs were high. Unemployment was high. Prices for goods were high. All of these things caused a **recession**.

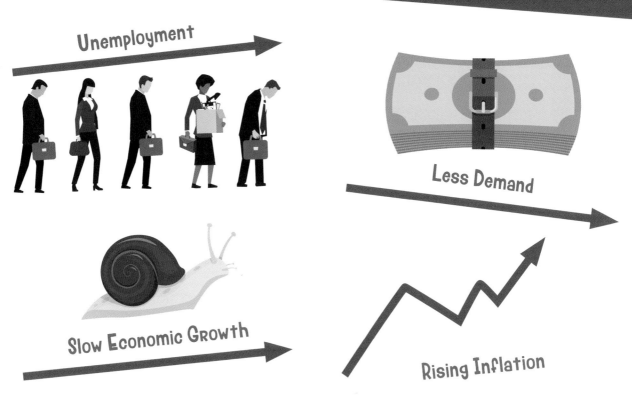

Unemployment

Less Demand

Slow Economic Growth

Rising Inflation

Parts of the Consumer Price Index (CPI)

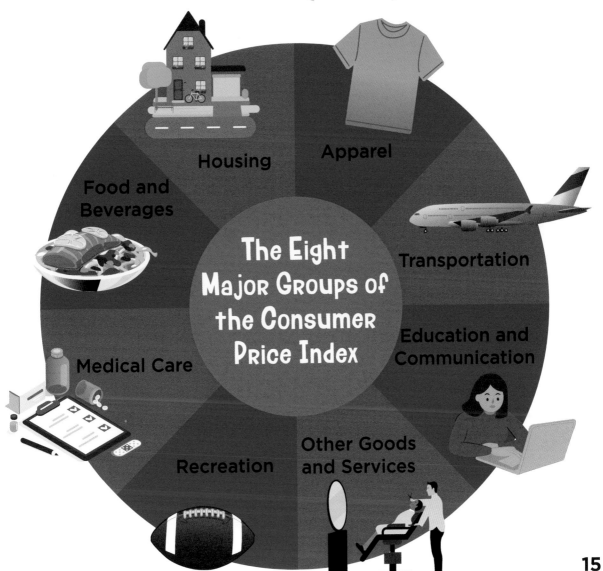

Housing

Apparel

Food and Beverages

The Eight Major Groups of the Consumer Price Index

Transportation

Medical Care

Education and Communication

Recreation

Other Goods and Services

Producer Price Index (PPI) Industries

Mining

Manufacturing

Forestry

The PPI for mining increased from 10.8% in April to 21.7% in May 2021.

Fishing

PPI Industries

Agriculture

The farm-level price received by producers for cattle rose 8.7% from January to August 2021.

Natural Gas and Electricity

Construction

Waste and Scrap Materials

Fast Facts

- **The United States has PPI reports for more than 535 industries and 4,000 products.**

- **The U.S. Bureau of Labor Statistics releases around 10,000 PPIs every month.**

The Value of a U.S. Dollar
(1800–2020)

$1 in 1800 is equal to about $22.06 today.

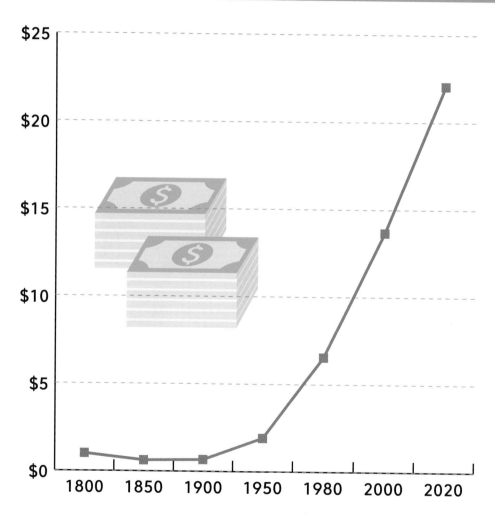

2022, CPI Inflation Calculator

INFLATION PROS AND CONS

It may seem like prices going up over time is a bad thing. But there are pros and cons to inflation. A steady inflation rate of around 2% is good. It shows that the economy is healthy. More money available means that more people have extra cash to spend. This means demand and production will go up.

Inflation can also help people who owe money. It is easier for them to pay back what they owe.

The Good and the Bad of Inflation

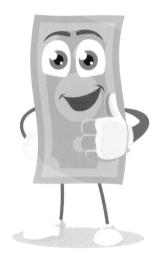

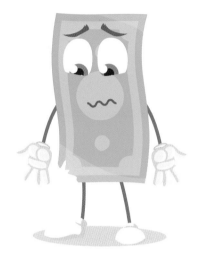

Pros

Economic growth

Wages go up

Prices go up

Less chance of a recession

Cons

Higher cost of goods and services

Unemployment rates may go up

The value of money goes down

People get less money if wages don't go up

U.S. Inflation Rates (2011–2021)

Inflation rates went up after the COVID-19 pandemic started in 2020. Prices went up due to less supply and more demand.

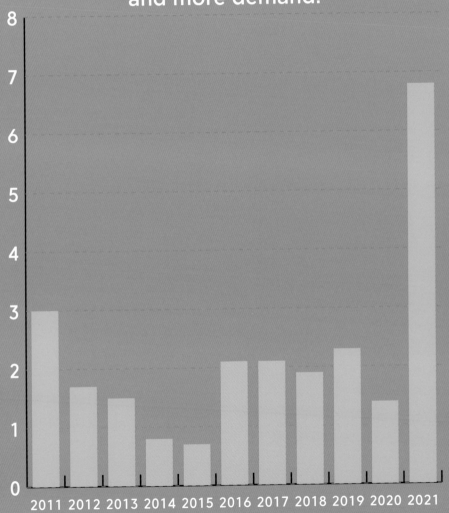

ACTIVITY
Calculate the Inflation Rate

How much has the price of your favorite chocolate bar gone up over time?

Create a bar graph with the following data:

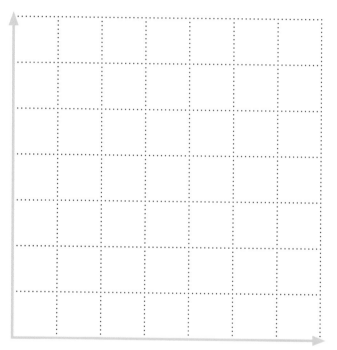

    1930: $0.05

    1940: $0.05

    1950: $0.10

    1980: $0.25

    2000: $0.75

    2010: $0.85

    2020: $1.00

You learn that the chocolate bar was first sold in 1920. But you don't have data for that year. What is a good guess for how much it cost then?

If the inflation rate in 2021 is 3%, how much will you pay for your chocolate bar?

Do you think the price will always go up? Why or why not?

What might make the price go down?

LEARN MORE

Books

Dakers, Diane. *Getting Your Money's Worth*. New York: Crabtree Publishing Company, 2017.

Sebree, Chet'la. *Understanding Inflation*. New York: Cavendish Square, 2020.

Websites

Britannica Kids: Inflation
https://kids.britannica.com/students/article/inflation/275058

Kiddle: Inflation Facts for Kids
https://kids.kiddle.co/Inflation

Bibliography

Dolasia, Meera. *"Why Venezuelans Are Paying Millions of Bolivars for a Cup of Coffee."* August 27, 2018. https://www.dogonews.com/2018/8/27/why-venezuelans-are-paying-millions-of-bolivars-for-a-cup-of-coffee

PBS Learning Media. *"The Lowdown: Understanding Inflation: A Stop Motion Explainer."* 2014. https://ca.pbslearningmedia.org/resource/mkqed-math-rp-inflation/understanding-inflation- stopmotion-explainer

Treebold, Jim. *"Inflation and the Future Value of Money."* March 31, 2018. https://www.encyclopedia.com/articles/inflation-and-the-future-value-of-money

GLOSSARY

consumers (kuhn-SOO-muhrz) people who buy goods and services

deflation (dih-FLAY-shuhn) decrease in the amount of available money or credit in an economy that causes prices to go down

demand (dih-MAND) desire to purchase goods and services

index (IN-deks) a number that indicates changes in the level of something when it rises or falls

inflation (in-FLAY-shuhn) continual increase in the price of goods and services

raw materials (RAW muh-TEER-ee-uhlz) basic materials used to make or create something

recession (rih-SEH-shuhn) period with less economic activity and fewer jobs available

wages (WAY-jez) amount of money that a worker is paid based on the time worked

INDEX

"Big Mac index," 6–7

Consumer Price Index (CPI), 13, 15

consumer prices, 4, 6–7, 8–9, 10–12, 13, 14, 15, 21

currency value, 13, 18, 20

deflation, 4–5

economic conditions, 14, 20

forecasting methods, 13

gaming consoles, 12

inflation, 4–5
  activities, 22
  cost-push, 8–9
  demand-pull, 10–12
  forecasting, 13
  illustrations, 6–7
  measures, 13, 16, 17
  pros and cons, 19–20
  rates, 18, 21, 22
  regional differences, 7

stagflation, 14
inventory issues, 10–11

Producer Price Index (PPI), 13, 16, 17

production factors, 8–9, 16

stagflation, 14

supply and demand, 4, 8–9, 10–12, 21

unemployment, 14, 20

wages, 8, 20